MW00883838

Prescriptive Analytics

Prescriptive Analytics

A SHORT INTRODUCTION TO
COUNTERINTUITIVE INTELLIGENCE

• • •

Andre Milchman
Noah Fang

Copyright © 2017 by Andre Milchman and Noah Fang

All rights reserved. No part of this publication may be reproduced, distributed, or transmitted in any form or by any means, including photocopying, recording, or other electronic or mechanical methods, without the prior written permission of the publisher, except in the case of brief quotations embodied in critical reviews and certain other noncommercial uses permitted by copyright law.

Prescriptive Analytics. A Short Introduction to Counterintuitive Intelligence / Andre Milchman and Noah Fang—First ed.
ISBN: 197992970X
ISBN-13: 9781979929707

Contents

About the Authors

•••

ANDRE MILCHMAN IS AN ENTERPRISE architect and a software developer. Originally trained in civil engineering, he worked as a construction engineer in the oil and gas industry. Following a path well-trodden by many in the 1990s, he received a degree in software engineering, then became a Sun Certified Enterprise Architect and worked as a software professional for various financial-services companies in Canada.

Andre is passionate about systems thinking, complexity science, social systems architecture, advanced analytics, and artificial intelligence. He is the author of Enterprise Architecture Reimagined: A Concise Guide to Constructing an Artificially Intelligent Enterprise and is a coauthor of the upcoming book The Transformable Enterprise. Andre currently lives in Toronto.

Noah Fang is a designer, business strategist, and pioneer of interactive storytelling. His past roles include creative director, user-experience manager, experience designer, product manager, editor, graphic designer, software engineer, and more. He has also translated three books on design and interactive storytelling. He studied computer science in college and was drawn to the broader field of design over the years. He lives with his family in Ottawa.

To Sean, Kaylee, and Nathan
—Andre

For Malinda and Marlene
—Noah

Making decisions is a routine part of business operations and often occurs with little thought about the decision-making process. In some cases, this may work well, considering the operational environment, but in other cases a structured approach may be required.

—RANDY E. CADIEUX

Frequently Asked Questions

• • •

Q: Could you tell me what prescriptive analytics is about in one sentence?

A: Prescriptive analytics crystallizes the reality of a specific situation and generates decisions that help human and artificial agents navigate that reality.

Q: There's already predictive analytics. Why do we need prescriptive analytics?

A: We can draw an analogy between the process of achieving some significant business goal with the process of navigating through a complex maze where more than one path can lead to the final point. In that case, predictive analytics predicts the final point in the maze, whereas prescriptive analytics generates the best strategy for navigating through the maze...but it doesn't draw a path through the maze.

Q: Why did you write this book?
A: The book wrote itself—unconsciously—into the mind of one of the authors four years after his creative experimentation with genetic algorithms. He shared it with his (future) coauthor, who offered his help in converting it into a book because the insight gained through the experimentation was general, interesting, and enlightening and can solve some pressing problems.

Q: Who is this book for?
A: The book is for believers, nonbelievers, and the undecided who find the concept of counterintuitive intelligence a significant one to explore and judge for themselves. It can help already convinced believers—analytics professionals with experience in software development and artificial intelligence—get up to speed with the prescriptive-analytics framework and build desktop or enterprise prescriptive-analytics applications. For people who are yet undecided on the subject of counterintuitive intelligence, the book will gradually help you understand the main concepts related to prescriptive analytics and the impact they will make on the future of business and life. Although nonbelievers may disagree with the ideas developed in this book, we would still like to show you what's possible when synergy is created between analytical capabilities of people and computational capacities of artificially intelligent machines.

Q: How this book will help me?
A: The book will help you (1) explore the problem space, solution space, and operational space of prescriptive analytics;

(2) understand the analytical and computational phases of generating decision sets (decision sets are the outcomes of prescriptive-analytics solutions); and (3) take advantage of emerging best practices in development and execution of the decision sets.

Q: After I finish this book, what's next?
A: There are a number of things you can do. First, explore use cases where prescriptive analytics can be applied today to set a foundation for your company's future. Does your company use robots, software agents, or smart objects that can take advantage of automatically generated decision sets? Are the effects of applying those decision sets computable and comparable? Second, try to model the situation applicable to the selected scenario, and identify viable alternatives. Finally, get your hands dirty: try to develop your first prescriptive-analytics application, and have some fun.

Q: How do I reach you guys when I have questions or different opinions?
A: Please don't hesitate to contact us through any of the following ways:

Andre
andre@method.org
Noah
noah@method.org
@kingofark on Twitter
www.kingofark.com

Introduction: Toward Exponential Wisdom

• • •

Contemporary futurists, industry executives, analysts, and consultants emphasize that we live in the world of Big Data. Very few talk about Big Information, and almost nobody talks about Big Knowledge and Big Wisdom. Why not? Because we don't know how to build the bridge between Big Data and Big Information to Big Knowledge and Big Wisdom. Why so?

Because we, human beings, rely too much on intuition:

Taking a straight line between A and B is intuitive.
Falling in love with and marrying a physically attractive woman or man is intuitive.
Sending kids to the best schools is intuitive.
Keeping up with the Joneses is intuitive.
Falling out of love and divorcing a physically attractive woman or man is also intuitive.

We don't learn to appreciate moderation. We want the simplest, the shortest, the cheapest, the most delicious, and the most beautiful. Intuition tells us to get the best.

Then what is not intuitive?

* Serendipitous accidents. Scottish scientist Alexander Fleming mistakenly left the dish containing Staphylococcus open in his laboratory, which led him to the discovery of a Penicillium mold. Other accidental inventions and discoveries include gravity (Sir Isaac Newton), anesthesia (Horace Wells), saccharin (Constantin Fahlberg and Ira Remsen), the high-power microwave beam (Percy Spencer), Teflon (Roy Plunkett), chewing gum (Thomas Adams), chicken cholera vaccine (Louis Pasteur and his assistants), and the list can go on and on.

* The results of systematic experimentation and development. Sometimes only hundreds or even thousands of highly focused prescriptive-analysis iterations can produce meaningful results that can never be realized intuitively. Historians Robert Friedel and Paul Israel list over twenty inventors of incandescent lamps prior to Thomas Edison, who made one thousand unsuccessful attempts at perfecting the bulb.

* The vision of genius. Newton's gravitational laws, Darwin's natural selection, Mendeleev's periodic table of elements, and Einstein's relativity theory are great examples of paradigm shifts in natural sciences that transformed entire societies, economies, and industries. What makes genius is the ability to climb the

shoulders of giants—to acquire, analyze, and systemize information—combined with the capacity to synthesize new knowledge.

It seems, however, that the times when we could either rely on random inventions or on genius to point in the right direction are over. Today, we can mostly rely on ourselves making great things together as a result of many iterations of hard work. Together is the key word here, because hard work wouldn't help much if humans were not social. The ability to leverage communication and coordination mechanisms explains the historical dominance of social insects and of humans who were able to compensate for the limited intelligence and capabilities of individuals with effective collaboration and cooperation within and between groups.

We succeed even more when we can construct wholes. These wholes include both small bounded wholes like hives, colonies, and families and higher-level wholes like tribes, communities, and nations. The process has been slow, uneven, and painful. It took human civilization thousands of years to build robust societies that sometimes don't destroy themselves and one other.

Over those years, humans together made trillions of trillions of decisions, big and small. That is why we are now exactly where we are.

Yes, we still want success that comes from luck. We still want those random, counterintuitive, and beautiful things that come to us as epiphanies or pure luck. But what we want even more is the success that comes from intentional, systematic, and often counterintuitive activities. We also want to delegate dull, dirty, and dangerous work to artificial autonomous agents—robots, virtual assistants, and smart objects. To operate autonomously, artificial agents need decisions.

Today, we can organize the mass production of high-quality, complex, and counterintuitive decisions that will be manufactured by artificial intelligence algorithms, which do exactly what nature does, but trillions of times faster.

The appetite for decisions is growing exponentially. Not only can humans execute decisions: artificial agents can now execute them on behalf of humans.

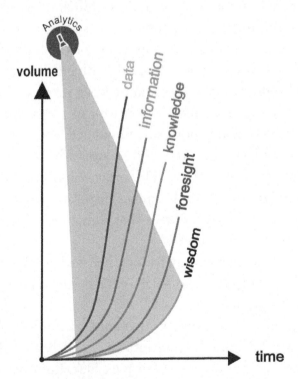

Figure 1. Analytics-driven push toward exponential wisdom.

Framing problems and generating complex and counterintuitive decisions is the mission of prescriptive analytics, which enable both analytics professionals and artificial intelligence algorithms to show their best. This is what the book is about.

●●●

Bad News and Good News

In business analytics, the recommended best practice is to deliver bad news first so that analysts can quickly get it out of the way and focus on the positive. We hereby deliver the bad news first: the combination of descriptive analytics, diagnostic analytics, and predictive analytics is no longer enough. Descriptive analytics will help you understand what happened; diagnostic analytics will help you understand why it happened; and predictive analytics will help you understand what will likely happen in the future. But the question still remains: Now what?

Figure 2. Taking advantage of four types of analytics.

There's a gap between what will happen and what we can do about it. Predictive analytics informs about the former, while the answer to the latter may not be as intuitive as it may seem at first.

Imagine that you could predict winning numbers—for example, 1, 2, 3, 4, 5, and 6—for the next lottery draw. How many tickets should you buy? In 1,000 Weeks of Lotto—What Worked, What Didn't. An In-Depth Statistical Analysis of 20 Years of Lottery Results, author Terry Fisher observes such an intriguing case:

> In a huge Florida Lottery Jackpot in 1990, over 52,000 people played 1-2-3-4-5-6 in a single week! Imagine sharing your prize with 52,000 other people—it would hardly be worth the trip to bank it. Other popular choices are all the 5s or all the 7s, e.g. 5-10-15-25-35-40. If you win the Lottery, you want as few winners as possible sharing the prize; ideally, just you. (Fisher 2006, 23)

However, for every bit of bad news, there is better news to tell. A new discipline of analytics—prescriptive analytics—has come to the rescue. As you can guess from the above example, prescriptive analytics don't offer descriptions, diagnoses, or predictions. The outcomes of prescriptive-analytics solutions are decisions: large, complex, and counterintuitive decision sets. Prescriptive analytics inform us of what we can do.

• • •

WHAT THE TRENDS REVEAL

Prescriptive analytics didn't come about in one day. There were revealing cues from the past that can help us understand the questions of "why this?" and "why now?"

Let's examine screenshots of Google Trends for two key phrases: prescriptive analytics and Internet of Things. (Google Trends is a powerful public tool from Google that provides insights into relative search volumes over time for a key word or phrase. It's accessible at google.com/trends.) The first screenshot shows the increasing popularity of the term prescriptive analytics in around 2012.

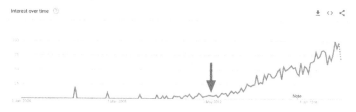

Figure 3. Google search trends for *prescriptive analytics*.

The next screenshot depicts a similar upward trend for the term *Internet of Things*.

Figure 4. Google search trends for *Internet of Things*.

Although it would be absolutely triumphant to show a similar trend for the term *robotics*, Google Trends shows that it has passed its peak of popularity of early 2000s.

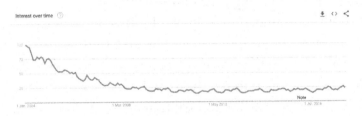

Figure 5. Google search trends for *robotics*.

Nevertheless, a decade ago, the most innovative companies started quickly closing the gap between research and practice in artificial intelligence. They began populating the world with intelligent robots and smart Internet of Things (IoT) objects, which pave the way for new multifaceted phenomena, such as smart cities, smart homes, and smart workplaces. McKinsey predicts:

> Now is the time to begin planning for an era when the employee base might consist both of low-cost Watsons and of higher-priced workers with the judgment and technical skills to manage the new knowledge "workforce." (Bughin, Chui, and Manyika 2013)

Humans can benefit from outcomes of prescriptive analytics solutions or decision sets, but because of decision sets' complexity, size, and counterintuitiveness, humans will not be able to execute them directly. They will use their judgement and guide the adaptive execution of those decisions by robots, personal assistants, software agents, and smart IoT objects.

Although many are concerned that robots will come and take humans' jobs, we believe that three characteristics will make people successful and indispensable in the future workplace. The first and most important characteristic is accountability: the fact that only humans can be held accountable for their actions logically positions them as strong centers surrounded by autonomous agents and smart objects in the future workplace (as shown on the below diagram). The second characteristic is the unique combination of social, physical, and computational capabilities that enables us to organize and manipulate both physical objects (to make) and representations of physical and abstract objects (to compute). The third characteristic is human touch, which will make future human services a premium offering.

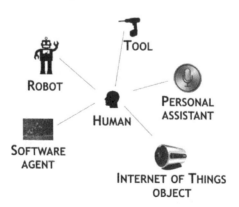

Figure 6. Humans are strong centers in the future workplace.

• • •

Why This Book

In the 2005 commencement address to Kenyon College, which some call the best commencement speech of all time (Jackson 2015), David Foster Wallace told a parable about three fish:

> There are these two young fish swimming along and they happen to meet an older fish swimming the other way, who nods at them and says, "Morning, boys. How's the water?" And the two young fish swim on for a bit, and then eventually one of them looks over at the other and goes "What the hell is water?" (Wallace 2005)

Figure 7. David Foster Wallace's three-fish parable.

That parable pretty much sums up the origin of this book. It's a story of becoming aware of the context. In the words of one of the authors:

In 2013, I was reading Chapter 9, "Genetic Algorithms," from Melanie Mitchell's book, Complexity: A Guided Tour. The author illustrated the concept of genetic algorithms by describing the adventures of her soda can–collecting robot named "Robby," who was trying to clean his computer-simulated, 100-square-foot, two-dimensional world, which was littered with empty soda cans. While reading the detailed description of Melanie Mitchell's solution, I suddenly had the idea of applying genetic algorithms to generating strategies for automatic currency trading. I took a one-year break from work and developed that application in 2014.

Although initially I was going to implement the idea as a plain Java console application, I later added a web interface, which put the application under pressure for continuous adaptation and improvement. After a few iterations, I looked at the solution and realized that it can be easily generalized to other problem spaces beyond financial services: robotics, logistics, and sports and entertainment were the first to come to mind.

Even though I was aware of Gartner's categorization of analytics into four categories (descriptive, diagnostic, predictive, and prescriptive analytics), I couldn't connect the dots. In 2014, I went back to work and never had a chance to monetize the software nor apply it to currency trading. Around the same time, I started reimagining the discipline of enterprise architecture and writing a book about the subject, so I wasn't thinking about the trading application for almost three years.

In 2017, I received an invitation to present my enterprise architecture framework at a quant (short for "quantitative analyst") conference in Toronto. Because I was concerned that the topic of enterprise architecture would not be relevant to quants, I looked at the currency-trading solution once again and finally had a moment of awareness and enlightenment: "This is prescriptive analytics."

This made me start thinking that I should not only present my findings at the conference but also should write a book to share what I had discovered while conceptualizing and developing the solution and some thoughts on how it can be improved. I discussed the matter with my friend and former colleague, and we came to conclusion the idea Is worth expanding into a book and decided to write the book together.

It appeared that the status quo was against writing the book, because we are not strictly the experts in this field. Our areas of expertise are enterprise architecture and design. However, despite the risk of looking incompetent, we decided to distill the most essential insight into a short book and hopefully open windows of understanding for nonexperts. We believe that elegant and simple prescriptive-analytics solutions have a potential to transform the workplace in various key industries, including yours.

The problem space of prescriptive analytics is transparent, logical, and clear. To define the space, we used the 5WH method by considering the who, why, where, what, when, and how of the problem. As we showed, it is agents—robots, personal assistants, software agents, and smart IoT objects—who take advantage of the outcomes of prescriptive analytics. During the future execution of their activity (when), agents will find themselves in various situations (where) and must make decisions (how) by choosing the best possible alternative action (what) for each situation.

Figure 8. The problem space of prescriptive analytics.

The goal of this book is to build a bridge from the problem space to a solution space and provide general recommendations on ways to develop a prescriptive-analytics platform. To enable analytics professionals and software developers to systematically produce prescriptive-analytics solutions, the authors present the *prescriptive-analytics framework* (PAF) that conceptualizes and structures problem space, solution space, and execution space of prescriptive analytics. The *problem space* of prescriptive analytics describes relationships in the real world, where the solution doesn't exist yet. Components of the prescriptive-analytics software, which enable analytics professionals to model and generate decision sets, belong to the *solution space*. Once the solution is in place, it starts sending decision sets to the *execution space*.

Some PAF components exist in all three spaces. In the problem space, they are not sufficiently formalized yet. Situations are often vague, imprecise, and not explicit. Not all possible alternatives are developed and parameterized. Decisions are often made without a clear understanding of goals and evaluation of potential consequences. Because of that, in today's problem space, decisions are mostly made manually by humans.

In the solution space, the decision factory comes into existence. Situations are modeled, alternatives are developed, and decision sets are generated and evaluated. Everything becomes machine readable and executable.

In the execution space, agents can precisely compute situations and find respective alternatives in decision sets. During the execution, agents take risk aspects, operational aspects, and other crosscutting aspects of the situation into consideration and can override the decisions recommended by prescriptive analytics if necessary.

Figure 9. Four areas of advanced analytics illuminated.

• • •

ORGANIZATION OF THIS BOOK

This book is divided into six chapters that help business-analytics professionals make sense of prescriptive analytics, structure prescriptive-analytics problems, and design prescriptive-analytics solutions.

Chapter 1, "Understanding Prescriptive Analytics," clarifies what prescriptive analytics is, lists high-potential use cases, and describes the most important characteristics of prescriptive analytics.

Chapter 2, "Constructing a Platform," proposes a three-layer design and describes solution components of the prescriptive analytics framework (PAF), which helps reduce the complexity of prescriptive analytics solutions.

Chapter 3, "Modeling Situations," explains the importance of situation awareness and shows how situations (detectable contextual characteristics of the problem) can be modeled so that solutions can be realized and refined according to specific contexts.

Chapter 4, "Developing Alternatives," defines the concept of decision alternatives (possible options that lead to a decision) and shows how they can be created and used for making decisions.

Chapter 5, "Computing Decisions," explains how prescriptive algorithms map situations to alternatives and describes how the process works.

Chapter 6, "Executing Decisions," describes two approaches—direct and adaptive—to executing decisions and explains the benefits of adaptive execution for agents operating in complex dynamic environments. We also discuss various agent activation mechanisms and how to apply John Boyd's OODA (observe, orient, decide, and act) Loop to executing decisions.

CHAPTER 1

Understanding Prescriptive Analytics

• • •

THROUGHOUT RECENT HISTORY, PEOPLE HAVE learned to take advantage of sophisticated analytical tools and methodologies for describing the past, diagnosing the present, and predicting the future with data. However, with the advancement of next generation artificial intelligence (AI) technologies, such as machine learning, natural language processing and generation, and AI-optimized hardware (among others), more powerful and better-equipped business analysts now face new challenges. Their abilities to describe, diagnose, and predict are no longer enough: they are now asked to prescribe the actions that should be taken not by humans but by robots, autonomous software agents, and smart Internet of Things (IoT) objects.

Prescriptive analytics has the power to shape the future. Descriptive analytics visualizes the past, diagnostic analytics explains the past, and predictive analytics explores the future. Prescriptive analytics takes data and metadata as the input, takes the purpose of the action in a focused way, produces complex decisions, and passes those decisions on for execution.

We summarize the differences between the four types of business analytics in the following table:

	Descriptive Analytics	Diagnostic Analytics	Predictive Analytics	Prescriptive Analytics
Focus	Hindsight	Insight	Foresight	Intent
Outcome	Data Reporting	KPIs Dashboards Alerts	Trends Behavior patterns Data scoring Forecasting	Decisions
Orientation	Past	Present	Future	Future
Techniques	Data aggregation Visualization	Data discovery Classification Culstering Correlation	Predictive modeling Machine learning Data mining	Situation modeling Option design AI algorithms

Figure 10. Comparison of the four areas of analytics.

Unlike descriptive, diagnostic, and predictive analytics, prescriptive analytics is a relatively new discipline still in search of its roots and is slowly gaining recognition in the field of business analytics.

Figure 11. Prescriptive analytics are now in fashion.

Every day, billions of people make trillions of decisions concerning all aspects of life and business. Although the impact of those decisions can be long-term and far-reaching—some can be a matter of life and death—most are based on our limited intelligence and experience and are rather simple and intuitive.

It is human nature to resist change and preserve the status quo, strive for clear rules and standards, and enjoy the harmony and conformity within a group. We are not capable of defining, evaluating, remembering, and executing complex decision logic.

In This I Know: Marketing Lessons from Under the Influence, Terry O'Reilly observes,

> The difficult thing about counterintuitive solutions is that they are often difficult to swallow and hard to present, and are usually shunned by almost everyone initially. They don't look or smell like past solutions. They don't resemble yesterday's answers. They often seemed hare-brained. You want to paint my chickens what colour? Yet the click you hear when opportunity, creativity and counterintuitive thinking lines up is unmistakable.
>
> To generate this kind of thought process, you have to shut out the status quo, standardized strategies and groupthink. Again, the phrase "That's the way we do it around here" is the death of marketing. If you want people to react to something in a new way, you have to communicate with them in a new way. If you want to solve a persistent problem, the answer just might have to be unorthodox. (O'Reilly 2017)

In contrast, prescriptive analytics generate, evaluate, and memorize complex decision sets that consist of hundreds or even thousands of decisions; pass them on for execution; and repeat these steps again as often as necessary.

To harness the immense capability of prescriptive analytics, an analytics professional needs to start by understanding their core concept and principles.

• • •

Defining Prescriptive Analytics

Many definitions of prescriptive analytics exist, including the one from Gartner's *IT Glossary*: "Prescriptive Analytics is a form of advanced analytics which examines data or content to answer the question 'What should be done?' or 'What can we do to make _____ happen?' and is characterized by techniques such as graph analysis, simulation, complex event processing, neural networks, recommendation engines, heuristics, and machine learning" (*Gartner IT Glossary* 2015).

On the other hand, Margaret Rouse provided the following definition, which more accurately reflects the essence of prescriptive analytics:

> Prescriptive analytics is the area of business analytics (BA) dedicated to finding the best course of action for a given situation. (Rouse 2012)

The following revised definition of prescriptive analytics replaces the word situation with set of situations and eliminates the word given, because modeling situations is an essential part of prescriptive analytics:

> Prescriptive analytics is the area of advanced analytics that takes advantage of machine learning algorithms to find the best course of action for a set of situations.

As a matter of fact, prescriptive analytics sits at the intersection of situation modeling, alternative design, and machine-learning algorithms.

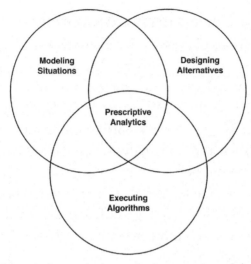

Figure 12. Prescriptive analytics at the intersection of three activities.

The outcome of prescriptive analytics should serve as an input to a generative execution process that achieves a certain goal, step-by-step, through a proper and creative unfolding process.

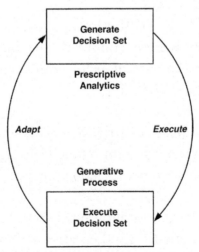

Figure 13. Two-phase cycle of prescriptive analytics.

During execution, generative processes face new circumstances, discover new possible courses of action, and refine their goals. Prescription analytics take this information into account and start the next cycle of adaptation. This core mechanism of prescriptive analytics borrows from and builds upon the philosophy of Christopher Alexander, who defined a generative development as an iterative, incremental, and adaptive process.

In his profound four-volume book, The Nature of Order, Christopher Alexander, the father of the pattern-language movement, argues that one million mistakes can be made (or avoided) when building a small community that consists of 150 houses. In this scenario, the number of potential mistakes corresponds to the sum of decision points contained in each house and the community plan as a whole.

Because building an average single-family house requires about two thousand on-site man-hours of labor, Alexander estimates that, for each house, construction workers—who make several decisions of position and dimension during each hour—face around five thousand decision points. Making these decisions by simply following general design guidelines contained in construction blueprints is no different than leaving them to pure chance or luck, in which case every decision will likely be a mistake. Investing mental effort, special attention, and deliberate thought in every decision is the only way to minimize the risk of mistakes.

Alexander further argues that the best solution for avoiding one million mistakes is using generative processes, each consisting of a steady series of small, careful adaptations that make up wholeness-extending transformations and continually refine the generated entity: "Generative processes tell us what to DO, what ACTIONS to take, step by step, to make buildings and building designs unfold beautifully, rather than detailed drawings which tell us what the END-result is supposed to be" (Alexander 2002).

He contrasts generated structures that gradually unfold in time with fabricated structures that come to existence "as an arbitrary accident which appears all at once, with no opportunity for correction or common sense" (Alexander 2002, 176):

> And the answer is, that there is a fundamental law about the creation of complexity, which is visible and obvious to everyone—yet this law is, to all intents and purposes, ignored in 99% of the daily fabrication processes of society. The law states simply this: ALL the well-ordered complex systems we know in the world, all those anyway that we view as highly successful, are GENERATED structures, not fabricated structures. (Alexander 2002, 180)

He illustrates this fundamental law with the example of the most complex neural network, the human brain, and other examples—such as Amazonian forests, the tiger, and the sunset over the western ocean—as analogies and highlights that generative processes, not fabrication or assembly, bring them into existence. These objects are too complex to have been products of fabrication or deliberate planning and design.

On the other hand, Alexander points to human genes as the way nature encodes the successful decisions made during the evolution of humankind and passes them to future generations:

A gene is an organism's way of remembering how to form previously successful adaptations in ensuing generations of new organisms. The gene essentially remembers, and allows re-use of, a generic solution to a recurring problem. In architecture, traditional pattern languages played the same role. When we build a house, or a door, or a path, or a garden, these words describe worked-out culturally defined generic centers—pattern-like concepts which can be generated in a thousand forms to make actual centers in the world. The good environments in traditional society could be built because people had pictures of what worked; these pictures were agreed upon, and used and re-used, over and again. (Alexander 2002, 346)

Although Alexander is talking about architecture instead of analytics, there are many profound similarities between the two when it comes to the general design principles. The outcome of the first analytical phase of prescriptive analytics is an encoded decision set computed using evolutionary algorithms. The operational (or execution) phase is a generative process that adapts the decision set to a specific context.

• • •

APPLYING PRESCRIPTIVE ANALYTICS

Generating high-volume decisions increasingly gives large and medium-sized enterprises a source of superior performance, differentiation, and competitive advantage.

Prescriptive analytics enable organizations to continually adapt to changing business conditions and gain a competitive edge to meet the challenges of the global business environment. High-potential use cases for prescriptive analytics include robotics, the IoT, fraud management, supply chain management, and investing and trading.

* **Robotics.** Today, robots operate in space, in the air, in water, on the ground, under the ground, and within the human body and in other biological environments. To successfully rescue people, defuse bombs, drive cars and tractors, inspect pipes, deliver packages, and prune and harvest crops, robots must not only continually make intelligent decisions based on sensory data from the environment, but must also use different decision sets when switching "attention."

* **Internet of Things.** Prescriptive analytics can enable smart IoT objects to make intelligent decisions when interacting with people and the surrounding environment. In addition, prescriptive analytics can help organizations manage their IoT-connected assets and connected operations.

* **Fraud management.** Prescriptive analytics can accelerate the process of adapting and updating fraud-detection models and generating rule sets that take

into account new patterns of fraud, thus complementing and gradually replacing legacy rule writing and outdated algorithms for risk scoring.

* **Supply chain management.** Because accurate and reliable data and information about logistics operations carried out by transportation and warehousing industries are available in real time, prescriptive analytics can help the field of logistics and supply chain management generate tactical and operational decision sets. Furthermore, it can help both to design new supply chains and to realign, readjust, and optimize existing supply chains and networks for dynamic change and growth.

* **Investing and trading.** Financial-services firms accumulate considerable volumes of trading, customer, and fundamental and technical market data, which enable them to begin using prescriptive-analytics solutions for trading and investing.

With the right descriptive, diagnostic, and predictive-analytics software, you can visualize the past, inform the present, and outline the future. And with prescriptive analytics, you can mass-produce decisions that make the future happen.

• • •

CHARACTERIZING PRESCRIPTIVE ANALYTICS

Once again, we face the dilemma of choosing between the problem-centric and the comprehension-centric approaches to analytics. Although this dilemma is also applicable to predictive analytics, prescriptive analytics takes it to the extreme because of the counterintuitiveness of outcomes.

Prescriptive analytics takes a problem-centric approach to analytics, thus sacrificing comprehensibility for effectiveness.

German philosopher Arthur Schopenhauer once said, "It is a clear gain to sacrifice pleasure in order to avoid pain." On a similar note, sometimes it is a clear gain to sacrifice comprehensibility to gain effectiveness and efficiency. However, when we don't fully understand something, we don't feel like we are in control. And, unfortunately, most of us are often willing to sacrifice great things to get more control.

The balance between analytics and intuition is subtle. In their best-selling book, Competing on Analytics: The New Science of Winning, Thomas H. Davenport and Jeanne G. Harris (2017) argue, "There is considerable evidence that decisions based on analytics are more likely to be correct than those based on intuition," although in situations when uncertainty is high and time pressure is great, relying on intuition may be the best option.

It's also clear that decision makers have to use intuition when they have no data and must make a very rapid decision—as in Gladwell's example of police officers deciding whether to shoot a suspect. Gary Klein, a consultant on decision making, makes similar arguments about fire-fighters making decisions about burning buildings. Even firms that are generally quite analytical must sometimes resort to intuition when they have no data. For example, Jeff Bezos, CEO of Amazon.com, greatly prefers to perform limited tests of new features on Amazon.com, rigorously quantifying user reaction before rolling them out. But the company's "search inside the book" offering was impossible to test without applying it to a critical mass of books (Amazon.com started with 120,000). It was also expensive to develop, increasing the risk. In that case, Bezos trusted his instincts and took a flier. And the feature did prove popular when introduced. (Davenport and Harris 2017, 14)

Intuition that leads to success usually makes sense when reflected back, while analytics often go against what we "feel" to be right. In Humans Need Not Apply: A Guide to Wealth and Work in the Age of Artificial Intelligence, Jerry Kaplan (2015) describes Amazon's highly efficient and effective—but counterintuitive to humans—way of storing products in warehouses, called chaotic storage:

For example, consider the way Amazon constantly adapts the stock patterns in its warehouses. If a person were to do the warehouse planning (as in many more traditional companies), products might be organized in a logical and comprehensible way—identical items would be stored next to each other, for example, so when you needed to pick one, you knew where it was. But a synthetic intellect of the sort Amazon has built isn't subject to this constraint. Like items can be located next to others that are frequently shipped with them, or on any shelf where they fit more compactly. To the human eye, it looks like chaos—products of different sizes and shapes are stacked randomly everywhere—which is why this type of warehouse organization is known as chaotic storage. But a synthetic intellect can keep track of everything and direct a worker to exactly the right place to fulfill an order far more efficiently than a human organizer could. (Kaplan 2015)

In some cases, the counterintuitive approach may be the only way to solve a problem. Terry O'Reilly describes a counterintuitive approach to driver safety taken by the city of Chicago:

The city of Chicago is built on the lip of a great lake. As a result, Chicago roads have a lot of dangerous winding S-curves hugging the lakeshore—which led to many traffic accidents. Clearly, the city needed to do something to lower the vehicle mishap rate.

First, it made the lane markings much more distinct. Nothing changed.

Then it made the curve-warning signs bigger. No one noticed.

Then it added big flashing lights on the curve-warning signs. Nothing worked.

So the city decided to expand its thinking beyond the usual solutions. And here's what Chicago did. It painted new horizontal stripes on these roads—beginning

> evenly spaced as usual—but as they get closer to the curve, it painted the stripes closer together.
>
> Why? Because it gives drivers the sensation they are driving faster. Why in the world would you want drivers to feel like they are driving faster when approaching an S-curve? Because the immediate instinct is to slow down. And when drivers slow down, fewer accidents occur. Make people think they are driving faster on S-curves to slow them down. I love that kind of thinking. It was a perfectly counterintuitive solution to a persistent problem. (O'Reilly 2017)

Besides being counterintuitive, prescriptive analytics have other characteristics that stand out as essential.

To summarize, high-quality prescriptive-analytics solutions are executable, explicit, directed, counterintuitive, adaptive, open-ended, and flexible.

* **Executable.** Robots, software agents, personal virtual assistants, smart objects, and sometimes even humans can execute outcomes of prescriptive-analytics solutions. When operating in the environment, they compute a situation, find a respective action for that situation in the decision set, and execute that action.
* **Explicit.** Unlike the decisions that are embedded in traditional software applications, the decisions that are produced by prescriptive-analytics software are expressed declaratively, which gives nonprogrammers explicit insight into the decision logic. To increase

readability, those decisions can be expressed as a set of natural language statements.

* **Directed.** Every focused execution of a situation-to-action mapping algorithm uses a fitness function or a value function as a performance criterion, which computes and compares the performance of thousands of decision sets.

* **Counterintuitive.** In most cases, humans won't be able to comprehend, memorize, communicate, and execute decision sets generated by prescriptive-analytics solutions. If intuitiveness is a desired characteristic of the outcome, one can program a directing function using intuitiveness as one of the performance criteria. An example of the difference this function could create would be well-organized storage that is highly intuitive for humans instead of chaotic storage that can be efficiently operated by robots. If intuitiveness is not used as a performance criterion, the prescriptive-analytics solution will lead the outcome in a different, sometimes opposite direction. In that case, the result will likely contradict common sense, conventional wisdom, daily experiences, and even beliefs of humans.

* **Adaptive.** Analytical steps of the two-step prescriptive-analytics process adapt decision sets to both changing aspects of the situation and changing decision options. For instance, when the robots that take advantage of prescriptive analytics are equipped with two additional sensors and four additional tools,

analysts can likely add two situation aspects and four alternatives to the solution.

* **Open-ended.** Because real-world applications usually have no time limits or boundaries and continuously generate new data, prescriptive steps of the two-step prescriptive-analytics process take advantage of that data and endlessly learn and produce a diversity of large, complex, and interesting decision sets. This enables executing agents to use decisions created by considering refined and more recent data.

* **Flexible.** Analysts can make focused executions of the solution by selecting not only relevant subsets of situation aspects and decision options, but also a specific fitness function and an optimizer. This flexibility enables executing agents to not only use highly focused decision sets, but also switch attention and take different sets of actions by using several decision sets at the same time.

Those characteristics can be used to guide the design and implementation of a prescriptive-analytics application or solution. They can also be used as a framework of analysis in the vendor evaluation-selection process.

• • •

Summary

Prescriptive analytics is the least-developed area of advanced analytics and is the area where analytics professionals usually spend the least amount of time. This situation will likely soon change with the rapid growth of artificial intelligence technologies and the Internet of Things, both of which quickly expand both the problem space and the solution space of prescriptive analytics.

The key takeaways from this chapter are the following:

* Prescriptive analytics is one of the four types of advanced analytics. The other three types are descriptive analytics, diagnostic analytics, and predictive analytics.
* Like predictive analytics, prescriptive analytics is oriented toward the future; its outcomes are decision sets that are meant to be executed by artificial agents.
* High-potential use cases for prescriptive analytics include robotics, the Internet of Things, fraud management, supply chain management, sports and entertainment, and investing and trading.
* High-quality prescriptive analytics solutions are executable, explicit, directed toward a certain goal, counterintuitive, adaptive, open-ended, and flexible.

CHAPTER 2

Designing a Platform

•••

PRESCRIPTIVE ANALYTICS PLAYS TO THE strengths of both humans and machines. It requires the synergy between the analytical capabilities of humans and the algorithmic capabilities of artificially intelligent software.

In his 1996 book, Cybercorp: The New Business Revolution, James Martin (1996) points out that "many decisions should not be made by humans alone or by software alone, but by a combination of the two" (173) and outlined the potential division of decision-making responsibilities between humans and machines that still remains relevant as a reference point:

> We need to understand clearly what decisions can be entrusted to software and what decisions must remain human decisions.
>
> *Decisions that are best left to machines include:*
>
> * Simple decisions (such as when to reorder goods)
> * Decisions that need complex but precise logic (such as allocation of gates to incoming flights at a large airport)

- Decisions that require logic so intricate that the human cannot compete with the computer (such as rescheduling of equipment after failures and delays on a large airline)
- Decisions that must be made too rapidly for human involvement (such as which trunk to use when routing packets over the Internet)
- Decisions that must be human decisions include:
- Decisions that are too subtle to program and need the special skills of human intelligence
- Decisions that need creativity, originality and intuition
- Decisions where human sensitivities predominate
- Business negotiation, including negotiating rules of encounter that can then be programmed (Martin 1996, 173)

Prescriptive-analytics problems are complex, and that complexity can be characterized in three dimensions: situation complexity, choice complexity, and decision complexity.

Situation complexity is limited only by the structure of human activity, which has no limits or boundaries.

Choice complexity is limited only by what's possible and what's impossible.

Decision complexity represents the prescriptive complexity of prescriptive analytics, which is part analytical and part computational.

Situation complexity and choice complexity comprise the analytical complexity of prescriptive analytics.

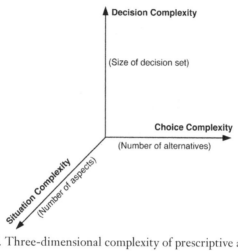

Figure 14. Three-dimensional complexity of prescriptive analytics.

• • •

TAMING PRESCRIPTIVE ANALYTICS

Dealing with the universe of all possible situations and courses of action is not only inefficient, but also highly impractical. To make the complexity manageable, we can logically partition prescriptive analytics software into three layers: a platform layer, an application layer, and a solution layer.

Accordingly, the three layers have their complexity scoped in each of the three prescriptive-analytics dimensions introduced in the previous section.

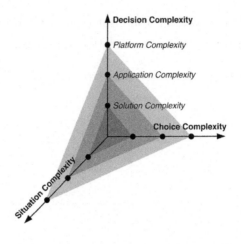

Figure 15. Platform, application, and solution layers help make the complexity of prescriptive analytics manageable.

The prescriptive-analytics software design is structured as a set of horizontal layers, which represent the logical division of functionality, not the physical distribution of components.

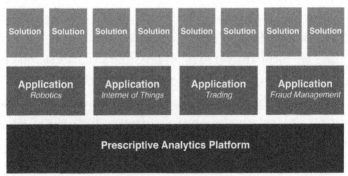

Figure 16. Three-layer design of prescriptive analytics software.

The two lower layers of this three-layer design are responsible for creating building blocks relevant to a problem domain. The top layer uses those building blocks to construct the solutions that can be executed by other artificial agents.

- **The platform** serves as a container for the prescriptive-analytics applications related to specific problem domains.
- **Applications** are responsible for identifying all aspects of situations, possible courses of action, and performance criteria for specific problem domains.
- **Solutions** take subsets of situation aspects and possible alternatives and generate the best decision set that satisfies the selected performance criterion.

Prescriptive-analytics platforms can be implemented as traditional web applications and deployed in the cloud as SaaS (software-as-a-service) platforms.

● ● ●

COMPONENTS OF THE PLATFORM
In the introduction, we briefly outlined a problem space of prescriptive-analytics framework (PAF). The following diagram shows a generalized solution space of PAF.

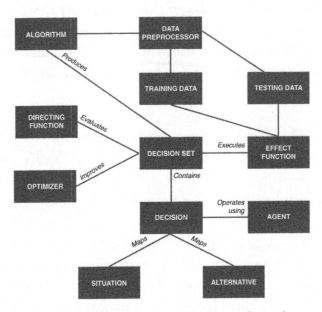

Figure 17. The solution space of prescriptive-analytics framework.

The solution space of PAF consists of the following components:

* **Situations** are defined as sets of aspects in which each aspect is defined either as a set of intervals or a set of discrete values that represent respective abstractions of the real-world problem situations.
* **Alternatives** are courses of actions that are relevant to a given situation and produce computable and comparable effects.
* **Algorithms** coordinate the process of generating, executing, and evaluating candidate decision sets; in the

end, they (1) identify the decision set that maps each situation to the best alternative, (2) optimize it, and (3) execute it against testing data sets.

* **Effect functions** execute decision sets against historical data sets; the result of each execution is passed as input to the respective directing function for evaluation.

* **Directing functions** represent performance criteria for each decision set and, as the name implies, lead the solution in the desired direction. Directing functions comprise the function library that is created for every application.

* **Training data sets** are used by mapping algorithms to generate rule sets or decision sets.

* **Test data sets** are used by mapping algorithms and test and validate generated decision sets.

* **Data preprocessors** compute the aspects of situations that are derived from the original data.

* **Optimizers** improve the quality of generated decision sets by, for instance, eliminating high-risk, insufficiently tested, or lower-performing choices. Optimizers comprise the optimizer library that is created for every application.

To initiate the prescriptive-analytics system, analysts should be able to construct component models using traditional web interfaces, visual modeling interfaces, or both.

• • •

Seven Recommendations on Designing Prescriptive Analytics Platforms

There are seven recommendations that can be used to guide the construction of a prescriptive-analytics platform. Unlike the outcomes of prescriptive analytics, these principles are simple, straightforward, intuitive, and easy to follow.

- **Take advantage of the hierarchical structure of the suite.** Use the platform as a container of domain-specific applications and applications as containers of prescriptive analytics solutions.

- **Model general (common) aspects of situations and courses of action at the platform layer.** All-purpose artifacts, such as temporal aspects of situations (e.g. *day of week* and *hour of day*), can be defined once at the platform layer and either plugged in or inherited by applications and solutions.

- **Create interfaces, superclasses, and default implementations at the platform layer.** Superclasses that contain directing and optimizing functions should be implemented at the platform and inherited by applications and solutions.

- **Define all relevant situation aspects and courses of action at the application layer.** That way, solutions can take advantage of any combination of aspects and alternatives. When working at the application layer, analysts should be guided by the MECE principle and ensure that aspects and alternatives for each application are mutually exclusive and collectively exhaustive ("MECE principle").

⁕ **Create reference focuses of attention at the application layer.** Each focus of attention will enable selective concentration on a discrete set of aspects. A solution will either leverage an existing reference focus of attention or create its own.

⁕ **Take advantage of the plug-in architecture pattern.** Implement situation aspects and respective intervals, alternatives, directing functions, and optimizers as pluggable components to your prescriptive-analytics algorithm.

⁕ **Visualize everything.** Make all components visible. This puts them under pressure for constant improvement. It would be also beneficial to visualize and analyze the execution of the prescriptive-analytics algorithm.

● ● ●

Summary

In this chapter, we explained how to design a platform that would enable the creation of many prescriptive-analytics solutions—a platform that would take advantage of both analytical capabilities of humans and algorithmic capabilities of artificially intelligent machines. There are four key takeaways:

- The three dimensions that determine the complexity of prescriptive-analytics problems are decision complexity, situation complexity, and choice complexity.
- Prescriptive-analytics software can be implemented as a web-based application that consists of three layers: (1) the platform layer that serves as a general container for domain-specific applications; (2) the application layer, where domain-specific aspects of situations, choices, and performance criteria are defined; and (3) the solutions layer, where decision sets are generated.
- The main physical components of the prescriptive-analytics framework are (1) situations, (2) alternatives, (3) algorithms, (4) effect functions, (5) directing functions, (6) training data sets, (7) test data sets, (8) data preprocessors, and (9) optimizers.
- The most important recommendations on designing software include the following: (1) effectively divide responsibilities between the three layers, (2) enable continuous improvement by visualizing both processes and outcomes, and (3) extensively use the plug-in architecture pattern.

CHAPTER 3

Modeling Situations

• • •

PRESCRIPTIVE ANALYTICS SOLUTIONS TELL US which situations we can take advantage of and which situations should be avoided. Analysts must be able to distinguish significant aspects of the situation and find ways to quantify them so that the situation becomes instantly, unambiguously, and clearly recognizable, and appropriate actions can be taken.

In their book *Designing for Situation Awareness: An Approach to User-Centered Design*, Mica R. Endsley and Debra G. Jones emphasize the importance of situation awareness (SA) in operating, collaborating, and interacting in complex dynamic environments:

> *The concept of SA is usually applied to operational situations, where people must have SA for a specified reason, for example in order to drive a car, treat a patient, or separate traffic as an air traffic controller. Therefore, SA is normally defined as it relates to the goals and objectives of a specific job or function.*

> *Only those pieces of the situation that are relevant to the task at hand are important for SA. While a doctor needs to know all of a patient's symptoms in order to diagnose an illness or ailment, the doctor does not usually need to know every detail of the patient's history. Likewise, the pilot of an aircraft must be aware of other planes, the weather, and approaching terrain changes, but the pilot does not need to know what the copilot had for lunch. (Endsley and Jones 2016, 13)*

Although the authors break down the definition of situation awareness "into three separate levels: Level I—perception of the elements in the environment, Level 2—comprehension of the current situation, and Level 3—projections of future status" (Endsley and Jones 2016), prescriptive analytics concentrates on situation design and, as we explained in the first chapter, does not require comprehension of the current situation. The outcome of a prescriptive-analytics solution can be a large and counterintuitive decision set, which can later be analyzed and understood with the aid of visualization software.

When defining situations, we point out that their aspects must be relevant to a purpose or a goal, but we would like to underscore that the goal itself cannot be considered an aspect of a situation. A situation is a combination of values of purpose-relevant detectable contextual characteristics (aspects) of the problem at a given time.

As follows from the definition, the characteristics that describe situations must have three traits:

* **Related to a problem.** As Endsley and Jones remarked, "The pilot does not need to know what the copilot had for lunch" (2016, 13). Although in most cases this aspect of a situation can be safely excluded, sometimes hidden connections can be discovered between this aspect and either other aspects of the situation or the choices the copilot (or even the pilot, who might not really appreciate the offensive odor of garlic on the breath of his crewmate) makes when operating the plane.
* **Contextual.** Aspects related to temporal, spatial, social, economic, political, and other contexts must be taken into consideration.
* **Relevant to a purpose or a goal.** Distinctly different goals (for instance, impact investing and socially responsible investing) require different subsets of aspects related to financial services.
* **Detectable and quantifiable.** One must be able to unambiguously compute the situation from its characteristics.

Analytics professionals must understand these characteristics and carry out both qualitative and quantitative analyses of situations.

• • •

Defining Aspects

Situation analysis begins with a qualitative analysis of factors affecting the problem at hand. We call these factors *aspects*. Because all aspects of the situation must be quantifiable, we must have data for each situation aspect. The data should be available, derivable, obtainable, and collectable.

* **Available.** For instance, your company can have historical intraday Forex rates, which include hourly opening, high, low, and closing prices and trading volumes for main currency pairs.
* **Derivable.** Moving averages, standard deviations, Bollinger Bands, relative strength indexes (RSI), and many other technical indicators can be computed using historical rates as the input.
* **Obtainable.** Nontraditional data sources are available today. For instance, modern cognitive computing systems, such as IBM Watson, can access and analyze massive volumes of structured and unstructured data and analyze financial sentiment based on news articles and social media postings, which can include general market mood (bullish vs. bearish), general levels of demand and supply, recommendations for financial instruments (buy or sell), and other sentiment categories.
* **Collectable.** In the case of robotics and the Internet of Things, situational-aspect data can be continually collected by various sensors and detectors during and between prescriptive-analytics cycles.

It's important to note that we must be able to combine aspect data by using common variables. In each data set, we must have at least one common variable that serves as a join key. Aspects can be organized into various groups—for instance, temporal aspects, spatial aspects, business aspects, social aspects, and so on. As we discussed previously, general aspects that can be used by many applications are defined at the platform layer; problem-specific aspects are defined at the application layer.

The qualitative analysis of situational factors is followed by a quantitative analysis, which partitions aspects into numeric intervals. It is desirable to partition aspects into the intervals that have business significance. For instance, for each currency pair in a foreign exchange trading application, the opening, trading, and closing hours of respective markets (for instance, London, New York, Tokyo, and Sydney sessions) are business significant.

In many cases, however, when defining intuitively meaningful intervals is impossible, analysts can use statistical methods, scrutinize and analyze every data sample, and use empirical evidence to identify conventionally meaningful zones of interest. An example of a situation aspect with such zones is a popular technical indicator, the Relative Strength Index (RSI), which was developed and introduced by J. Welles Wilder in his book *New Concepts in Technical Trading Systems*. RSI is a momentum oscillator that always swings back and forth between zero and one hundred. According to the traditional interpretation, the values around fifty represent neutral market momentum, values under thirty represent oversold markets conditions, and values above seventy represent overbought conditions (Wilder 1978). Later interpretations use RSI readings below twenty to indicate oversold conditions and readings above eighty to indicate overbought conditions, which creates the opportunity to further refine and partition the twenty-to-eighty zone and assign meaning to new intervals.

The following diagram shows how a situation created at the solution layer can be composed of subsets of general aspects defined at the platform level and subsets of domain-specific aspects defined at the application layer. The solution situation doesn't use all aspect intervals but instead selects only those of interest.

The solution selects only one day of week (Friday), two hours of day (8:00–9:00 a.m. and 9:00–10:00 a.m.), three intervals of standard deviation, four intervals of RSI, two intervals of volume, and three intervals of sentiment.

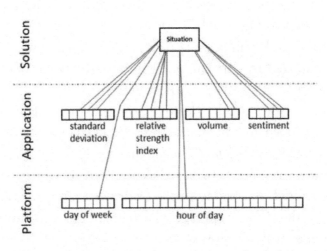

Figure 18. Situation represented as a set of aspects divided into intervals.

Based on this, we can calculate the number of possible situations that can occur during execution. This number corresponds to the size of the computed decision set that will map every situation to one of possible alternative actions.

$1 \times 2 \times 3 \times 4 \times 2 \times 3 = 144$ situations

This means that the decision set produced by a prescriptive-analytics solution for this particular scenario will always contain 144 decisions.

• • •

Five Recommendations on Situation Modeling

The following five recommendations can be used to guide situation modeling.

* **Expand situation boundaries.** Using social network data in credit scoring is an emerging practice at many companies that try to distill business insights from massive volumes of data generated by social media. Although this practice is considered controversial (because, on the one hand, it threatens the privacy rights and freedom of consumers, and, on the other hand, consumers can strategically construct their social profiles to get better scores), it provides an excellent example of how seemingly unrelated factors show high correlation.

❧ **Assign domain-specific meaning to general aspects.** Redefine the general platform-layer aspects at the application level. For instance, a general hour-of-day aspect defined at the platform level can be redefined as the market hour of day in the trading application.

❧ **Define mutually exclusive and completely exhaustive aspects and ranges of aspects at the application layer. Establish selective focus at the solution layer.** This will enable executing agents to change guiding decision sets when selectively switching the focus of attention and limiting it to small subsets of aspects and ranges of aspects.

❧ **Strive to break each aspect down into a set of intervals that are significant to the problem domain.** The usage of precise and meaningful intervals will greatly increase the quality of the final decision set.

❧ **Use machine-learning, statistical, and empirical methods to identify classes, clusters, thresholds, and neutral and extreme zones.** One interesting example of such effort is the famous and widely used classification of a normal distribution of innovation adopters (innovators, early adopters, early majority, late majority, and laggards) introduced by Everett Rogers—who synthesized research from over five hundred diffusion studies—in his book *Diffusion of Innovations* (Rogers 1962).

Partitioning aspects into meaningful intervals is the most labor-intensive and time-consuming part of the situation-modeling process. Leveraging classification and clustering machine-learning algorithms for aspect partitioning will reduce manual work and improve the quality of situation models.

•••

Summary

Two analytical tasks—situation modeling and developing alternatives—are essential for structuring a prescriptive-analytics problem. In this chapter, we emphasized the importance of situation awareness and, consequently, detailed and systematic situation modeling for prescriptive analytics.

The key takeaways:

* Identifying and quantifying domain-significant aspects of the situation is the key prescriptive-analytics activity that most markedly affects the quality of generated decision sets.

* During the execution of a prescriptive-analytics decision set, an agent must be able to instantly and unambiguously compute the current situation and find it in the decision set based on its aspects and respective intervals.

* The situation model is supported by data that must be either available, derivable, obtainable, or collectable at both design time and run time.
* Both situation aspects and the respective intervals defined for a domain should be mutually exclusive and completely exhaustive (the MECE principle), meaningful, and domain specific.

CHAPTER 4

Developing Alternatives

• • •

IN THE PREVIOUS CHAPTER, WE looked at the circumstances relevant to the situation; in the present chapter, we need to identify what's possible given the goal and the situation. We call those possibilities *alternatives.*

In *Words of Wisdom: A Thinker's Palette*, Scott Gallagher cites the words of Saint Francis of Assisi: "Start by doing what's necessary; then do what's possible; and suddenly you are doing the impossible" and then comments:

> If we can discover what it is we need to do, then we will see that it is possible, possible because it is necessary. The difficulty lies in that first step, the discovery. Mainly we do not do what is necessary for not knowing what is necessary to do. Once we see what needs to be done we've conquered the greatest obstacle. Then when we begin doing what is necessary the possibilities grow and grow until finally what we would have thought at the outset to be impossible is mysteriously at hand. This is why it is important to begin by doing

> *only what's necessary in the beginning so as not to give up before you even get started. (Gallagher 2010, 60)*

Way too often, decision makers make premature decisions without developing and evaluating alternative options, either because we don't have enough time to do it or because we don't have the capacity to do it. Fortunately, machines are exceptionally wise with time and have huge processing capacity. Identifying real or hypothetical alternatives is a critical analytical step—something that must be done before executing decision algorithms.

The inspirational words of Saint Francis of Assisi, "Start by doing what's necessary; then do what's possible; and suddenly you are doing the impossible," have become our simple three-step strategy for discovering alternatives.

• • •

Start with What's Necessary: Discovering Basic Alternatives

Always begin by identifying basic alternatives that are essentially relevant to the problem. In many cases, there are three basic options: the one that implies no action and a pair of contradictory alternatives, for example, *buy* and *sell* in the case of trading.

These three options are sufficient to create a basic prescriptive-analytics solution. In the example case of trading, the decisions are about how many units to buy or sell, when to close the transaction, or whether to do nothing at all.

• • •

CONTINUE WITH WHAT'S POSSIBLE: PARAMETERIZING ALTERNATIVES

The usage of basic options, such as *buy* and *sell*, doesn't mean that the respective actions are not parameterized. It simply means that prescriptive-analytics solutions are configured to use default parameters. In the trading example, "buy" actions can be executed as "buy" and close in 360 minutes, buy 10,000 units, and buy and close once the price drops by 1 percent or climbs above 2 percent. In the future, we will call the latter "buy" with stop-loss equal to 1 percent and take profit equal to 2 percent.

However, the solution can include both basic and parameterized actions, which can be configured for each execution. For example, the set of alternatives for an execution can consist of the following fifteen options:

Do Nothing
Buy (executed with the default configuration)
Sell (executed with the default configuration)
Buy and close in y minutes
Buy and close in (2 × y) minutes

Sell and close in y minutes
Sell and close in (2 × y) minutes
Buy z units
Buy (3 × z) units
Sell z units
Sell (3 × z) units
Buy with stop loss equal to m% and take profit equal to n%
Buy with stop loss equal to (1.5 × m)% and take profit equal to (1.8 × n)%
Sell with stop loss equal to m% and take profit equal to n%
Sell with stop loss equal to (1.5 × m)% and take profit equal to (1.8 × n)%

Other types of parameterized actions can also be added if the required data is available. Some possibilities are "buy" and "sell" actions with trailing stops. (When the price moves in a favorable direction, trades with trailing stops move the stop-loss level at the same pace in the same direction, thus enabling the trade to continue to gain in value.) However, this can significantly increase the execution time.

● ● ●

CONSIDER THE IMPOSSIBLE: USE INTERESTING COMBINATIONS AND WILD CARDS

The moment of truth is reached when all reasonable possibilities are exhausted and only unreasonable, impractical, impossible, and beyond-impossible options remain.

In his book, *How to Create a Vegan World: A Pragmatic Approach*, Tobias Leenaert (2017) gives some examples of disruptive vegan startups that successfully "develop alternatives that could potentially topple entire sectors of the animal foods industry":

> *The solutions these companies arrive at are often hi-tech. Here are a few of them:*
>
> * *Impossible Foods is developing the ideal plant-based burger.*
> * *Beyond Meat does the same as Impossible Foods: their Beyond Chicken and Beyond Burger products are already in Whole Foods markets.*
> * *New Wave Foods is trying to create synthetic shrimp from algae.*
> * *Hampton Creek is working to take egg-laying hens out of the food chain by developing egg alternatives. Hampton has been successful at branding and marketing its Just Mayo vegan mayonnaise.*

- *Clara Foods has a similar mission as Hampton Creek, but is even more hi-tech. It's working on the world's first animal-free egg white, and is a division of IndieBio, the world's first synthetic biology accelerator, located in San Francisco.*
- *Perfect Day wants to produce a product that is chemically, nutritionally, and tastewise identical to milk, based on cow DNA but with otherwise no cow involved.*
- *Memphis Meats in Silicon Valley has already created the first meatball from cultured meat.*
- *In the Netherlands, the famous Vegetarian Butcher is a young company with the ambition of becoming the biggest "butcher" in the world. In just a couple of years' time, the company is selling its products in four thousand outlets in fifteen countries. The Vegetarian Butcher works together with the world-famous agricultural university in Wageningen and the technical University in Delft to engineer and accelerate technological breakthroughs. (Leenaert 2017)*

Reaching (and even looking) beyond what is possible today and tomorrow is tough, but it is necessary in order to overcome limits of what prescriptive analytics can achieve in the future. Some interesting options may include the following:

- Actions with interesting combinations of parameters
- Composite actions (e.g., buy and hedge)

* Actions with wild card parameters (in this case, the algorithm will have to compute a more precise parameterized action for each situation, e.g. *buy* and close in 233 minutes or *sell* 1987 units).

Thinking beyond impossible breaks the barriers of traditional patterns and forms and assists in pushing the envelope to explore the future of counterintuitive intelligence. Although most of the attempts may end up fruitless, it's the very act of exploring those "impossibilities" that affords the innovative new ground. It's also important to remember that, whereas humans find experimenting as time-consuming, effort intense, and often not even feasible, AI-powered machines have no trouble doing it in a time-wise and cost-effective manner. By making possible what's impossible to us humans, we can discover new possibilities.

• • •

FIVE RECOMMENDATIONS ON DEVELOPING ALTERNATIVES

Whether we are looking at the Internet of Things or robotics, business or logistics, sports or art, it is clear that we need to develop a completely exhaustive set of valid, viable, and effective alternatives so that prescriptive-analytics algorithms can select a subset of possible situations and map them to a subset of possible alternatives, thus creating a set of executable decisions.

The following principles can guide the development of alternatives for a prescriptive analytics solution.

- **Always include a default alternative.** This should be the one that produces zero or few harmful or undesired effects.
- **Each alternative must have a computable effect.** The choice must be executable by the decision algorithm and compute a result.
- **Effects must be comparable.** The decision algorithm must be able to compare results produced by all alternatives.
- **Introduce qualitatively different parameterization options.** Consider using temporal, spatial, business, and other parameters.
- **Explore the impossible.** Continually introduce new challenges that would make you relentlessly search for better data, better models, and better algorithms.

Figure 19. Consider using pronounceable names for alternatives.

Both developers of prescriptive-analytics solutions and those responsible for the execution of decision sets must iteratively adjust, develop, and test new alternatives based on continual feedback from one other.

• • •

SUMMARY

Developing feasible, diverse, and complete alternatives is the second essential analytical task that helps structure a prescriptive-analytics problem. The analyst's goal is not only to identify an initial set of intuitively obvious alternatives, but also to look beyond what is possible today.

Key takeaways:

* Determining what's possible given the goal and the situation is another central activity critical to the success of any prescriptive-analytics project.
* The prescriptive-analytics framework (PAF) distinguishes two types of alternatives: basic and parameterized. When executing the former, effect functions apply default execution parameters.
* Analytics professionals can also experiment with advanced options, such as using (1) interesting combinations of parameters, (2) composite actions, and (3) actions with wild card parameters.
* The most important recommendation is to always include the default alternative that produces no harmful or undesired effects.

CHAPTER 5

Computing Decisions

• • •

PRESCRIPTIVE ANALYTICS LEVERAGES MACHINE INTELLIGENCE to generate decisions that will be mostly executed by machines such as robots, artificial software agents, and smart (IoT) objects. Humans will not be able to execute the decisions produced by prescriptive-analytics solutions because of the size and complexity of their outcomes.

Prescriptive analytics is not only an artificially intelligent technology by nature. The success of prescriptive analytics will bring other AI technologies to the state-of-the-art level.

Silicon Valley's recent explosion of artificial intelligence startups scares many celebrities, wealthy magnates, and even scientists. The following is how James Barrat explained why he wrote his book, *Our Final Invention: Artificial Intelligence and the End of the Human Era*:

> *I've written this book to warn you that artificial intelligence could drive mankind into extinction, and to explain how that catastrophic outcome is not just possible, but likely if we do*

not begin preparing very, very carefully now. You may have heard this doomsday warning connected to nanotechnology and genetic engineering, and maybe you have wondered, as I have, about the omission of AI in this lineup. Or maybe you have not yet grasped how artificial intelligence could pose an existential threat to mankind, a threat greater than nuclear weapons or any other technology you can think of. If that's the case, please consider this a heartfelt invitation to join the most important conversation humanity can have. (2013, 16)

In contrast, we look at artificial intelligence as just another tool in the toolkit of human strengths. Maybe today is the right time to stop seeing ourselves as "dwarfs standing on the shoulders of giants" ("Standing on the shoulders of giants," 2017) and start seeing ourselves as dwarfs standing on the shoulders of both giants and robots.

•••

Preprocessing Data

"In God we trust. All others must bring data," said W. Edwards Deming, an American visionary, system thinker, engineer, statistician, author, and management consultant best known as the architect of Japan's twentieth-century in-dustrial-quality revolution.

When creating a prescriptive-analytics application, a key challenge is to maximize data quality. Data preprocessing is usually performed at the application layer, so the data can be reused by many prescriptive-analytics solutions.

Data should be preprocessed for the following reasons:

* To compute values for derived aspects (for instance, technical indicators);
* To compute common variables (join keys) to merge various data sets; and
* To reduce the level of noise that can lead to overfitting to the data.
*

Data must be reprocessed when (1) new data sets are added or (2) new aspects are added at the application or platform layers.

• • •

Computing the Decision

The authors investigated a few possible machine-learning algorithms. In the end, we decided to use genetic algorithms as a core of our prescriptive-analytics software, mainly because the power, flexibility, and simplicity of their fitness functions can lead prescriptive-analytics solutions in the desired direction.

To generate a decision set that maps situations to alternative actions, one needs to configure ten elements.

* **A subset of situation aspects and a subset of intervals for each aspect.** They can be selected from the

general aspects and the respective intervals, defined at the platform level, and domain-specific situation aspects and respective intervals, defined at the application level.

* **A subset of alternatives.** These, too, can be selected from general and domain-specific alternatives defined at both levels. Multiple alternatives can be configured for parameterizable alternatives (e.g., [1] *Buy* and close in 120 minutes and [2] *Buy* and close in 180 minutes).

* **An effect function** can be selected from the function library and plugged into the execution.

* **A fitness function** can be selected from the function library and plugged into the execution.

* **An optimizer (or a chain of optimizers)** can be selected from the optimizer library and plugged into the execution;

* **A training data set** is selected from the list of available datasets;

* **Testing data sets** are selected from the list of available datasets that are related to the training dataset;

* **A size of a population of candidate solutions (population_size).** In genetic algorithms, the evolution begins with the initial population of the configured size. This and each successive population are called *generations.*

* **A maximum number of generations (max_generations).** The algorithm will iteratively execute the evolution *max_generations* times, or (if *stop_if* is

configured) will stop if there is no improvement in fitness for *stop_if* consecutive generations.

* **Stop if not improved (stop_if).** The execution stops when the algorithm reaches the limit of performance improvement.

To explain the execution of a prescriptive-analytics algorithm, we will use the following configuration based on the situation modeling example from Chapter 4:

Configuration of the Algorithm Execution

(1) Situation Aspects
* One *day of week* (Friday)
* Two *hours of day* (8–9:00 a.m. and 9–10:00 a.m.)
* Three intervals of *standard deviation*
* Four intervals of *relative strength index*
* Two intervals of *volume*
* Three intervals of *sentiment*

(2) Alternatives
To keep it simple, we select three basic alternatives.
* *Do Nothing* encoded as 0
* *Buy* encoded as 1
* *Sell* encoded as 2

(3) Fitness Function
We select the *MinNumberOfTradesFitnessFunction* that rewards both the maximization of trading profits and the minimization of number of transactions.

(4) Optimizer

We select the *BasicOptimizer* that finds the situations that didn't occur during the execution and resets the respective alternatives to Do Nothing.

(5) Training Data Set

We select hourly foreign exchange rates for the euro/US dollar currency pair for year 2015.

(6) Testing Data Sets

We select foreign exchange rates for the euro/US dollar currency pair for years 2010, 2011, 2012, 2013, 2014, 2016, and 2017.

(7) Population Size

population_size = 100

(8) Maximum Number of Generations

max_generations = 300

(9) Stop If Not Improved

stop_if = 50

Genetic algorithms aim to generate sufficiently good solutions to domain-specific problems by manipulating genetic representations of solutions. In the case of prescriptive analytics, the desired solution is a decision set, and a genetic representation of the solution is a bit string representation of integers called a *chromosome*. In a prescriptive-analytics chromosome, each index within the bit string corresponds to the index of a situation in the list of all possible situations, and the integer itself represents the alternative mapped to that situation.

In our example, we can calculate the number of possible situations by multiplying the number of intervals selected for each situation aspect:

$1 \times 2 \times 3 \times 4 \times 2 \times 3 = 144$ situations

The result is 144 possible situations, where each situation is a unique combination of six selected aspects. The below diagram shows the chromosome that represents 144 situations, which are not yet mapped to alternatives.

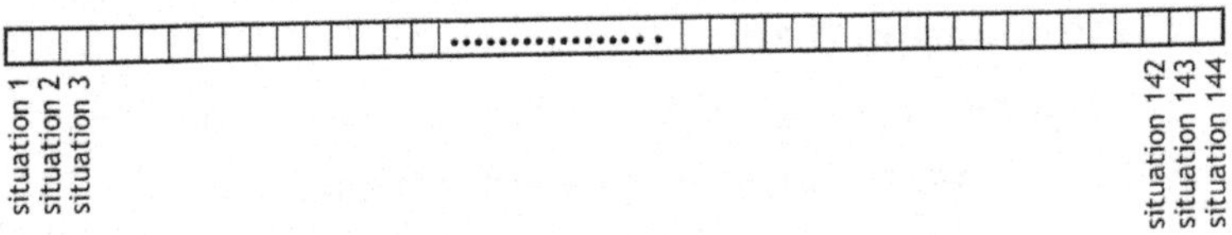

Figure 20. Empty solution chromosome.

The following diagram depicts the chromosome in which each situation is mapped to the DoNothing alternative. Because in most cases the execution of this chromosome (decision set) will have no effect, the fitness function should return zero.

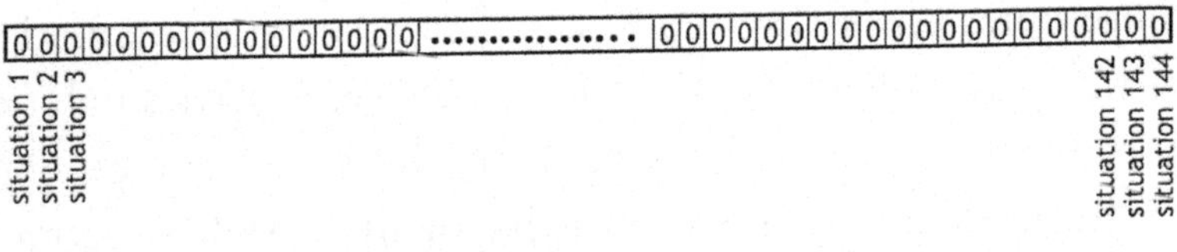

Figure 21. Solution chromosome with alternatives mapped to situations.

Prescriptive Analytics

With both the configuration and genetic representation of the solution defined, the prescriptive-analytics algorithm proceeds with the following steps.

* **Step 1. Create a population of randomly generated chromosomes.** In our case, the algorithm will generate the initial population of 100 random chromosomes (*population_size* = 100).

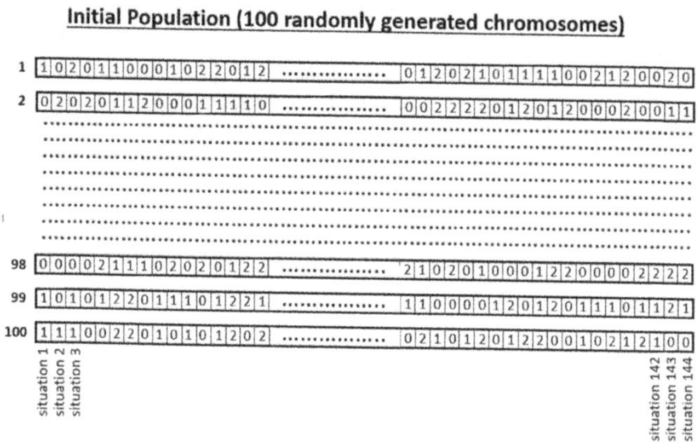

Initial Population (100 randomly generated chromosomes)

Figure 22. Initial population of randomly generated candidate solutions.

* **Step 2. Evaluate the fitness value of each chromosome in the population.** The algorithm sequentially applies decision sets encoded in each of the one hundred chromosomes to a historical data set (euro/US dollar currency pair for year 2015) by running two functions: a backtest engine and a fitness function. First, the backtest engine executes

55

a process called *back testing* (or *simulation* or *hind-casting*) by iterating through the historical data set and, for each record, (1) identifying a situation, (2) finding that situation in the chromosome, and (3) executing the respective alternative (because we didn't select parameterized alternatives, the engine simply closes "buy" and "sell" transactions in three hours). After completing these steps for all records, the backtest engine produces the result that serves as an input for the fitness function (in our case, MinNumberOfTradesFitnessFunction), which computes the fitness value of the chromosome.

* **Step 3. Generate the next generation population.** The algorithm selects the fittest chromosome and executes a combination of genetic operators—crossover and mutation—to generate the next generation's population of chromosomes.

* **Step 4. Execute the remaining process of evolution.** The algorithm executes the combination of Step 2 and Step 3 for the remaining 298 generations (we configured max_generations = 300) or stops the process if there is no improvement achieved after executing 50 consecutive generations (we configured *stop_if* = 50).

* **Step 5. Identify the fittest chromosome (decision set).** The algorithm selects the fittest chromosome of the last generation population for further optimization.

The fittest chromosome (decision set)

| 2 | 1 | 2 | 0 | 1 | 2 | 2 | 0 | 0 | 0 | 1 | 0 | 2 | 2 | 2 | 2 | .... | 0 | 1 | 1 | 0 | 1 | 2 | 2 | 1 | 2 | 2 | 0 | 0 | 0 | 0 | 2 | 2 | 2 | 1 | 1 | 1 |

situation 1
situation 2
situation 3

situation 142
situation 143
situation 144

Figure 23. The fittest chromosome.

- **Step 6. Optimize the fittest chromosome.** As we showed previously, some situations that were defined in a chromosome might never occur in the historical data set. The following diagram illustrates this case: even though the fittest chromosome mapped two situations (#1 and #130) with zero occurrences to *Sell* (value = 2) and one situation (#142) with zero occurrences to *Buy* (value = 1), the effect of those actions was never tested during the execution.

The fittest chromosome before optimization

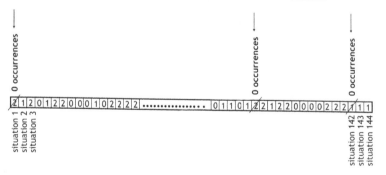

Figure 24. The fittest chromosome before optimization.

To reduce the risk that these three mappings can cause in production, the BasicOptimizer (that we configured for this algorithm execution) resets the alternatives mapped for situations #1, #130, and #142 to *DoNothing* (value = 0), as depicted below:

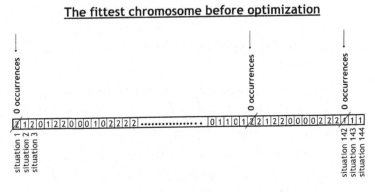

Figure 25. The fittest chromosome after optimization.

* **Step 7. Testing.** The algorithm applies the optimized chromosome to seven testing data sets (euro/US dollar currency pair for years 2010, 2011, 2012, 2013, 2014, 2016, and 2017).

If fitness values computed by the prescriptive-analytics algorithm by applying the fittest chromosome to testing data sets are in the same ballpark (within the expected general range), then the decision set can be considered sufficiently good and passed on as the candidate solution for adoption in a production environment. Otherwise, the solution most likely suffers from one of the two main problems of the solutions based on machine learning—overfitting or underfitting.

• • •

Is Every Problem a Gift?

Author, motivational speaker, and communication expert Anthony Robbins once said, "Every problem is a gift—without problems, we would not grow." Although in many cases it is true, some problems related not only to prescriptive analytics in particular, but also to machine learning in general, are not the kind of gifts of which one can never have enough.

A prescriptive-analytics solution can suffer from two systematic and distinct problems: overfitting and underfitting.

Figure 26. To end up at the podium, one must beat overfitting and underfitting.

Limited training data, excessive noise levels in data, and unrealistic goals and objectives encoded in directing (fitness) functions often lead to the well-known problem of overfitting, which results in decisions that are too specific and perform well on the training data set, but fail to generalize and produce desired outcomes when applied to the whole problem domain. Although overfitting is considered a nightmare of machine learning, some techniques can help reduce the overfitting risk. For instance, the eight guidelines proposed by Igor Tulchinsky in *Finding Alphas: A Quantitative Approach to Building Trading Strategies* are a good example: (1) creating true out-of-sample tests, (2) using longer history data sets, (3) making the model elegant (theoretically sound), (4) using fewer model parameters, (5) visualizing, (6) recording the number of trials, (7) testing on some artificial data sets, and (8) using dynamic models (Tulchinsky 2015).

Unlike overfitting, underfitting is easier to detect and deal with, because it usually cannot demonstrate the performance even on training data sets. If the algorithm cannot discover any patterns, trends, or relationships in a training data set, then the analyst should add situation aspects and selected alternatives with higher prescriptive importance and thus avoid oversimplifying and bringing the complexity of the solution to a practical level.

Figure 27. Prescriptive-analytics
professional in action.

● ● ●

SUMMARY

Whereas situation modeling and developing alternatives contribute to structuring the problem, the tasks that we described in this chapter—preprocessing data, directing with fitness functions, and optimization—contribute to the success of the prescriptive-analytics solution.

Let us wrap up the chapter by summarizing the key takeaways:

* Data preprocessing is an important activity that aims to maximize data quality and compute derived values.

It is usually performed at the application level, so the data can be reused by many solutions.

* To generate a decision set, an analytics professional can take advantage of the plug-in architecture pattern and select (1) a subset of situation aspects and a subset of intervals for each aspect, (2) a subset of alternatives, (3) a fitness function, (4) an optimizer, (5) a training data set, and (6) a test data set that were defined for the domain. She can also configure the characteristics specific to the machine-learning algorithm, for instance, a size of a population of candidate solutions and a maximum number of generations, in the case of genetic algorithms.

* The PAF's process of computing decision sets typically (1) creates a population of randomly generated chromosomes (decision sets), (2) evaluates the fitness value of each chromosome in the population, (3) generates the next-generation population, (4) executes the remaining process of evolution, (5) identifies, and (6) optimizes the fittest chromosome (decision set), and, finally (7) tests it on multiple test data sets.

* If the final decision set doesn't pass tests, the likely cause is its overfitting or underfitting the data. The poor performance can usually be explained by low-quality situation and alternative models.

CHAPTER 6

Executing Decisions

• • •

Humans benefit directly from outcomes of descriptive, diagnostic, and predictive analytics and indirectly from outcomes of prescriptive analytics. Because humans cannot execute large, complex, and counterintuitive decision sets produced by prescriptive analytics solutions, they delegate the execution to robots, software agents, virtual assistants, smart IoT objects, and politicians.

Figure 28. Politicians will be taking advantage of prescriptive analytics.

The role of humans in executing a prescriptive-analytics solution is not limited to passing the decision set to an agent for *direct execution* and monitoring its performance. Although this approach can work in simple settings with deterministic outcomes, we need a more sophisticated approach for the agents that operate in complex dynamic environments, which we call *adaptive execution*.

Figure 29. The victim of the direct execution approach.

It can take several iterations to adapt an agent to a decision set and an environment. During those iterations, execution analysts work with agents with gradually decreasing degrees of involvement, which can, for instance, follow the path defined by automotive engineers for autonomous vehicles: "hands on," "hands off," "eyes off," "mind off," and "driverless" (Blain 2017). While analyzing the execution, analysts refine the execution code by adding general rules that address various risks, safety, security, and other crosscutting concerns. Analysts can also override decisions recommended by prescriptive analytics.

During execution, agents respond to changing conditions in the surrounding environment by executing OODA (observe, orient, decide, and act) loops. OODA loops were proposed by US Air Force Colonel John Boyd as a way of achieving competitive advantage in aerial battles between fighter aircraft, but they were adopted and utilized far beyond military operations.

•••

Learning from Colonel Boyd

The whole world is now crazy about OODA loops, and we are no exception.

Figure 30. The world is crazy about OODA loops.

Roger Sessions described John Boyd's development of his theory of the OODA loop in his book, *Simple Architectures for Complex Enterprises*:

> Boyd was interested not just in any dogfight, but specifically in dogfights between MiG-15s and F-86s. As an ex-pilot and accomplished aircraft designer, Boyd knew both planes very well. He knew the MiG-15 was a better aircraft than the F-86. The MiG-15 could climb faster than the F-86. The MiG-15 could turn faster than the F-86. The MiG-15 had better distance visibility.
>
> There was just one problem with all of this. Even though the MiG-15 was considered a superior aircraft by Boyd and most other aircraft designers, the F-86 was preferred by pilots. The reason it was preferred was simple: in one-on-one dogfights with MiG-15s, the F-86 won nine times out of ten. (Sessions 2008, 48)

The detailed analysis of pilots' actions led Boyd to the conclusion that every dogfight is essentially a series of cycles, and during each cycle, pilots perform four distinct steps. Boyd called these steps "observe, orient, decide, and act" and introduced the term *OODA loop* for the whole.

However, the question still remained: Why does the F-86 consistently outperform the more advanced the MiG-15? This answer was not obvious to many:

> Boyd decided that the primary determinant to winning dogfights was not observing, orienting, planning, or acting

> *better. The primary determinant to winning dogfights was observing, orienting, planning, and acting faster. In other words, how quickly one could iterate.* Speed of iteration, Boyd suggested, beats quality of iteration.
>
> *The next question Boyd asked is this: why would the F-86 iterate faster? The reason, he concluded, was something that nobody had thought was particularly important. It was the fact that the F-86 had a hydraulic flight stick whereas the MiG-15 had a manual flight stick. (Sessions 2008, 49)*

John Boyd's OODA loop provides an effective framework for designing a sophisticated process of execution of prescriptive-analytics decision sets. The following section explains the process in detail.

• • •

EXECUTING OODA LOOPS

Autonomous agents operate in complex dynamic environments by executing OODA loops in response to events. The execution can be any of the following:

* **Event based.** Agents listen and respond to domain-specific events.
* **Time-based** or **schedule-based.** Agents get activated and execute OODA loops according to a schedule.

- **Location-based.** Agents respond when they detect a change of location.
- **Exception-based.** Agents respond to events triggered by exceptions.
- **Randomly prompted.** Agents are randomly activated to perform nonregular activities such as inspecting the environment, creating the appearance that someone is home, or ensuring that something (or someone) is still functioning.
- **Hybrid.** A combination of the above.

In the latter case, when required to respond to several types of events, an agent can be equipped with several sets of decisions.

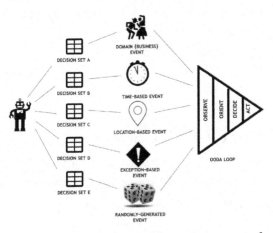

Figure 31. Agents can be activated by various types of events.

Let's consider time-based execution of a decision set using the example of a currency trading agent that we introduced previously.

Let's suppose the agent receives a decision set produced by a prescriptive-analytics platform for execution in a real environment. The following diagram shows the beginning and the end of that decision set:

#	Aspect 1	Aspect 2	Aspect 3	Alternative
1	<=30	>=0 and <=4	<-1.5	Buy
2	>30 and <=40	>4 and <=6	<-1 and >=-1.5	Do nothing
3	>40 and <=47	>6 and <=8	<-0.5 and >=-1	Buy
4	>47 and <53	>8 and <=10	<0 and >=-0.5	Buy
5	>=53 and <60	>10 and <=15	==0	Do nothing
....	....	....	....	....
....	....	....	....	....
143	>=60 and <70	>15	>1 and <=1.5	Sell
144	>=70	>=0 and <=4	>1.5	Sell

Figure 32. An example of a decision set sent for execution.

Because the decision set was created and tested on hourly euro/US dollar data sets, the agent will execute an OODA loop every hour during active foreign exchange market hours. Let's look at the OODA steps the agent will need to take at the beginning of any hour (*hour N*):

* **Step 1. Observe.** The agent activates, collects necessary data, and detects the following values of situation aspects that are relevant to the decision set:

  Aspect 1 (A1) = 65
  Aspect 2 (A2) = 17
  Aspect 3 (A3) = 1.2

This step is completed only when values for all aspects are retrieved or computed.

* **Step 2. Orient.** The agent finds the respective situation in the decision table.

#	Aspect 1	Aspect 2	Aspect 3	Alternative
1	<=30	>=0 and <=4	<-1.5	Buy
2	>30 and <=40	>4 and <=6	<-1 and >=-1.5	Do nothing
3	>40 and <=47	>6 and <=8	<-0.5 and >=-1	Buy
4	>47 and <53	>8 and <=10	<0 and >=-0.5	Buy
5	>=53 and <60	>10 and <=15	==0	Do nothing
143	>=60 and <70	>15	>1 and <=1.5	Sell
144	>=70	>=0 and <=4	>1.5	Sell

Hour N
Aspect 1 (A1) = 65
Aspect 2 (A2) = 17
Aspect 3 (A3) = 1.2

Figure 33. Finding the situation in the decision set.

In our case, aspects (A1 = 65, A2 = 17, A3 = 1.2) correspond to the situation #143;

* **Step 3. Decide.** The agent discovers that the best course of action for the situation #143 is *Sell*.

#	Aspect 1	Aspect 2	Aspect 3	Alternative
1	<=30	>=0 and <=4	<-1.5	Buy
2	>30 and <=40	>4 and <=6	<-1 and >=-1.5	Do nothing
3	>40 and <=47	>6 and <=8	<-0.5 and >=-1	Buy
4	>47 and <53	>8 and <=10	<0 and >=-0.5	Buy
5	>=53 and <60	>10 and <=15	==0	Do nothing
143	>=60 and <70	>15	>1 and <=1.5	Sell
144	>=70	>=0 and <=4	>1.5	Sell

Hour N
Aspect 1 (A1) = 65
Aspect 2 (A2) = 17
Aspect 3 (A3) = 1.2

Figure 34. Identifying the best course of action for the situation.

70

Although *Sell* is generally considered to be the best option to execute for the situation #143, the implementation of the "decide" step can be more complex than simply taking the decision provided by the decision set. For instance, the agent can apply the rule that cancels a *Sell* decision if previously executed sell transactions are still open.

❧ **Step 4. Act.** In our case, however, the agent executes a *Sell* transaction, and this completes the OODA cycle.

The following diagram shows that at the beginning of the next hour, the agent encounters a situation that corresponds to the situation #144 and the respective *Sell* action, which can be canceled, because of the above-mentioned rule. An hour later, the agent has to execute a *DoNothing* action that corresponds to situation #5.

Hour N	#	Aspect 1	Aspect 2	Aspect 3	Alternative
Aspect 1 (A1) = 65	1	<=30	>=0 and <=4	<-1.5	Buy
Aspect 2 (A2) = 17	2	>30 and <=40	>4 and <=6	<-1 and >=-1.5	Do nothing
Aspect 3 (A3) = 1.2	3	>40 and <=47	>6 and <=8	<-0.5 and >=-1	Buy
Hour N+1	4	>47 and <53	>8 and <=10	<0 and >=-0.5	Buy
Aspect 1 (A1) = 90	5	>=53 and <60	>10 and <=15	==0	Do nothing
Aspect 2 (A2) = 3					
Aspect 3 (A3) = 1.8					
Hour N+1					
Aspect 1 (A1) = 59	143	>=60 and <70	>15	>1 and <=1.5	Sell
Aspect 2 (A2) = 11	144	>=70	>=0 and <=4	>1.5	Sell
Aspect 3 (A3) = 0					

Figure 35. Every hour, the agent faces a new situation and takes a respective action.

This example illustrates that in some situations, adaptive execution that takes into consideration current conditions can be more effective than direct execution of the decision recommended by the prescriptive-analytics solution.

● ● ●

Five Recommendations on Executing Decisions

In most cases, it takes several iterations to adapt a prescriptive-analytics solution to a real-world application.

The following general recommendations can guide the execution of a prescriptive analytics solution.

* **Use direct execution only in simple environments.** In these environments, as situations should be well-defined and present no risk, outcomes of actions should be certain, and execution of any additional rules is simply not necessary.
* **Use adaptive execution to address risk and operation management.** Not all concerns were taken into consideration during the prescriptive-analytics phase. Some factors and actions that can produce harmful effects on objects in the environment or the agents themselves, as well as those related to the overall performance of the agents, are generally not considered in prescriptive analytics and, therefore, must be addressed during execution.

* **Take time to gradually increase autonomy of agents.** Initially, an agent can simply present decisions to humans who not only press the "approve" button, but also learn from the execution, identify the risks, and program the rules. During the next iteration, the agent can take over the process, but humans can retake control on the agent's request. Finally, the agent take full control over execution, whereas humans only monitor overall performance and receive alerts without focusing on details.

* **Choose appropriate event mechanisms.** Whereas responding to domain-specific events can be the most suitable approach for robotics and IoT scenarios, it could result in too many transactions in the currency-trading scenario, for which we decided to use time-based events. Using a combination of event mechanisms and multiple decision sets can add flexibility to your execution.

* **Use OODA loops to respond to changing conditions.** During the first step (observe), agents can detect changes in the surrounding environment, including the aspects that were not considered during the prescriptive-analytics phase. In the second step (orient), agents not only compute the situation and find the respective decision, but they also raise yellow and red flags that may indicate the presence of risk factors. During the third step (decide), agents assess and weigh the risks, apply general rules, and make the final decision. The last step (act) is when agents execute the final decision.

Thus, we need adaptive execution, flexible event mechanisms, and effective OODA loops.

● ● ●

Summary

Even the best prescriptive-analytics decision set cannot be considered successful without proper execution by an autonomous agent in a real-world environment. Before executing a decision set in a real environment, two important questions must be addressed. First, how much autonomy should we give to the agent? Second, how do we want the agent to detect changes in the environment?

Let's have a quick look at a few key takeaways from this chapter:

* Prescriptive-analytics decision sets are meant to be executed by artificial agents (robots, software agents, virtual assistants, and smart IoT objects) mostly in complex, dynamic environments.
* In simple environments where outcomes are certain, agents can execute them directly (direct execution).
* In complex environments, humans must adapt agents by addressing risks and other concerns that were not taken into the consideration by prescriptive analytics (adaptive execution).
* Agents get activated using event-based, time-based, location-based, exception-based, randomly prompted,

and hybrid mechanisms. They then compute the current situation and execute the respective decision. The decision can be overridden by the rules programmed during the adaptation.

* John Boyd's OODA (observe, orient, decide, and act) loop provides an effective framework for executing a decision.

CONCLUSION

• • •

WE HAVE ESTABLISHED THAT PRESCRIPTIVE analytics are about analyzing data, modeling situations, identifying alternatives, and executing artificial intelligence algorithms to generate large, complex, and precise sets of decisions. The combination of human intelligence and computational brute force of machines caused a breakthrough in business analytics and became a real game changer for the field.

We've come a long way together. Consolidating all that we have discussed so far, we can draw the following diagram (a 5WH diagram) that presents a big-picture view of prescriptive analytics.

The diagram shows that analytics professionals (*who*) take center stage in prescriptive-analytics activities such as modeling situations, developing alternative options, designing effect and value functions, and preparing data (*what*). Analytics professionals have the power to unleash a new wave of innovation in artificial intelligence (*how*).

Early success stories are generating new demand (*why*) for prescriptive analytics. Gartner Inc., a research and advisory firm, expects the prescriptive analytics software market to surpass $1.5 billion by 2021 and estimates that by 2018, "decision optimization will no longer be a niche discipline but a best practice in leading organizations to address a wide range of complex business decisions" (Hare, Woodward, and Swinehart 2017).

In his LinkedIn article "Why Prescriptive Analytics Is the Future of Big Data," Mark van Rijmenam points out that prescriptive analytics is now successfully used by a number of businesses in different industries (*where*) around the world:

> *General Electric (GE) and Pitney Bowes forged an alliance to leverage prescriptive analytics using data produced from Pitney Bowes' shipping machines and production mailing. GE developed customized applications for asset performance management (APM) for Pitney Bowes with its Pedix software platform so that Pitney Bowes could offer job scheduling capabilities and productivity and client services to its enterprise clients. PopSugar, a lifestyle media company, also uses prescriptive analytics to produce engaging content that its readers will find relevant and valuable. The company uses prescriptive analytics to understand its audience better and business value drivers. For instance, PopSugar was able to determine from 231,000 social shares and 7 million views that childhood nostalgia and recognizable product names helped increased social shares and readership (van Rijmenam 2017).*

To answer the when question, we queried Google Trends. Because we have an unwritten and unspoken agreement with Google that it only show trends, and we can interpret them any way we want to, we have come to the conclusion that the right time to take advantage of this rising discipline of analytics is now (*when*). The Great Robotics Revolution is around the corner. The Internet of Things transforms all industries by turning every object into a connected device. Digital technologies have reached the plateau of productivity. The appetite for automated decisions will grow exponentially.

In almost any business, prescriptive analytics opportunities provide significant potential for return on intelligent investment. To ensure the company is best positioned to capitalize on these opportunities, one needs to place equal emphasis on both development and creative and adaptive execution of prescriptive analytics solutions.

So grab your analytical kayak, a prescriptive paddle, and algorithmic gear, and go experience the beauty the prescriptive-analytics reefs have to offer.

EPILOGUE: DO WE NEED TO UNDERSTAND WHY IT WORKS?

• • •

PEOPLE ARE CONCERNED ABOUT HOW they can use large, complex, and counterintuitive automated decisions produced by prescriptive analytics if they don't understand *why* they work.

That's actually a very scientific question from which we can derive two propositions: First, do we have to always understand how and why they work if they consistently produce desired results without harmful effects? Maybe, while we should know that most of the working sciences we take for granted every day were established based on experiments and results, with or without fundamental theories to explain why they work. Perhaps another question worth asking is this: Do we have to know the absolute truth (assuming it exists) before we make use of the facts derived from it? Second, even if we are satisfied with performance, we still must find ways of monitoring the process, understanding execution

81

patterns, and providing useful feedback to analytics professionals. There are several areas where we can get help from other disciplines of advanced analytics.

* **Visualization.** Use tools and techniques of descriptive analytics to visualize execution flow at both design time and runtime.
* **Expectations.** Use tools and techniques of predictive analytics to set realistic goals and objectives, and code them in fitness functions.
* **Insight.** Use tools and techniques of diagnostic analytics to understand patterns that may lead to hypotheses about why it works.

All four types of advanced analytics—descriptive, diagnostic, predictive, and prescriptive—must work in concert for wisdom to get well settled on its exponential rails. Descriptive analytics help us understand relationships between facts. Diagnostic analytics help us understand the nature and cause of facts. Predictive analytics help us set goals. Prescriptive analytics help us navigate the maze of the problem space.

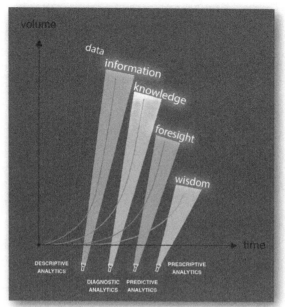

Figure 37. Toward exponential wisdom.

Perhaps we don't always need to understand why it works if it does. We simply must adequately manage risks, especially for mission-critical applications. However, if cost and time permit, it is worth it to make an effort to understand the patterns of execution. It's up to us to make the best of the art and the science of prescriptive analytics.

BIBLIOGRAPHY

•••

Alexander, Christopher. 2002. *The Nature of Order: An Essay on the Art of Building and the Nature of the Universe, Book 2: The Process of Creating Life.* Berkeley, CA: Center for Environmental Structure.

Barrat, James. 2013. *Our Final Invention: Artificial Intelligence and the End of the Human Era.* New York: St. Martin's Press.

Blain, Loz. 2017. "Self-Driving Vehicles: What Are the Six Levels of Autonomy?" *New Atlas*, June 7, 2017. https://newatlas.com/sae-autonomous-levels-definition-self-driving/49947/.

Bughin, Jacques, Michael Chui, and James Manyika. 2013. "Ten IT-Enabled Business Trends for the Decade Ahead." *McKinsey Quarterly*, May 2013. https://www.mckinsey.com/industries/high-tech/our-insights/ten-it-enabled-business-trends-for-the-decade-ahead.

Davenport, Thomas H., and Jeanne G. Harris. 2007. *Competing on Analytics: The New Science of Winning.* Boston: Harvard Business Review Press.

Endsley, Mica R., and Debra G. Jones. 2016. *Designing for Situation Awareness: An Approach to User-Centered Design.* London: CRC Press.

Fisher, Terry. 2006. *1,000 Weeks of Lotto—What Worked, What Didn't. An In-Depth Statistical Analysis of 20 Years of Lottery Results.* Bond University, QLD, Australia: LottoMasta International.

Gallagher, Scott. 2010. *Words of Wisdom: A Thinker's Palette.* *Charleston, SC:* BookSurge Publishing.

Gartner IT Glossary. 2015. "Prescriptive Analytics." Gartner. https://www.gartner.com/it-glossary/prescriptive-analytics.

Hare, Jim, Alys Woodward, and Hai Hong Swinehart. 2017. *Forecast Snapshot: Prescriptive Analytics, Worldwide.* Gartner. https://www.gartner.com/doc/3698935/forecast-snapshot-prescriptive-analytics-worldwide.

Jackson, Abby. 2015. "This Might Be the Best Graduation Speech of All Time." *Business Insider.* http://www.businessinsider.com/the-best-commencement-speech-of-all-time-2015-4.

Kaplan, Jerry. 2015. *Humans Need Not Apply: A Guide to Wealth and Work in the Age of Artificial Intelligence.* New Haven, CT: Yale University Press.

Leenaert, Tobias. 2017. *How to Create a Vegan World: A Pragmatic Approach.* Herndon, VA: Lantern Books.

Martin, James. 1996. *Cybercorp: The New Business Revolution.* New York: Amacom.

Mitchell, Melanie. 2009. Complexity: A Guided Tour. Oxford and New York: Oxford University Press.

O'Reilly, Terry. 2017. *This I Know: Marketing Lessons from Under the Influence.* Toronto: Knopf Canada.

Rogers, Everett M. 1962. *Diffusion of Innovations.* New York: The Free Press of Glencoe.

Rouse, Margaret. 2012. "What Is Prescriptive Analytics?" *SearchCIO—TechTarget.* http://searchcio.techtarget.com/definition/Prescriptive-analytics.

Sessions, Roger. 2008. *Simple Architectures for Complex Enterprises.* Redmond, WA: Microsoft Press.

Tulchinsky, Igor. 2015. *Finding Alphas: A Quantitative Approach to Building Trading Strategies.* Hoboken, NJ: Wiley.

van Rijmenam, Mark. 2017. "Why Prescriptive Analytics Is the Future of Big Data." *LinkedIn*. October 3, 2017. https://www.linkedin.com/pulse/why-prescriptive-analytics-future-big-data-mark-van-rijmenam/.

Wallace, David Foster. 2005. "Transcription of the 2005 Kenyon Commencement Address." https://web.ics.purdue.edu/~drkelly/DFWKenyonAddress2005.pdf.

Wikipedia. "MECE Principle." 2017. Accessed July 31, 2017, https://en.wikipedia.org/wiki/MECE_principle.

Wikipedia. "Standing on the Shoulders of Giants." 2017. Accessed October 10, 2017, https://en.wikipedia.org/w/index.php?title=Standing_on_the_shoulders_of_giants&oldid=79604419.

Wilder, J. Welles. 1978. *New Concepts in Technical Trading Systems*. Greensboro, NC: Trend Research.

Made in the USA
Las Vegas, NV
29 March 2022

46505476R00069